P9-DHK-238

May 2011
LYNNFIELD PUBLIC LIBRARY
LYNNFIELD, MASS. 01940

LYNNFIELD PUBLIC LIBRARY
LYNNFIELD, MA 01940

Saving Audie

A Pit Bull Puppy Gets a Second Chance

Dorothy Hinshaw Patent   photographs by William Muñoz

Walker & Company
New York

The black puppy shivered in the woods, chained tightly to an old car axle. He didn't know it, but he was facing almost certain death at Bad Newz Kennels. He'd either die in a dogfight or be killed for losing one. All he did know was loneliness and fear, thirst and hunger.

After dark came the worst. That's when the fights were held. Above the shouts of the human crowd, he could hear the snarls, growls, and yelps of the dogs who were forced to fight. He could smell the fear.

Life changed quickly for all the dogs at Bad Newz Kennels on April 25, 2007.

The government had found out about the illegal dogfighting and came to stop it. Strangers took the dogs away to animal shelters. They were held as evidence against NFL quarterback Michael Vick and his partners at the kennel.

But the lives of the dogs were still in danger. At that time, dogs taken from dogfighting outfits were kept as evidence until any trials were over, then put to sleep. People thought they would be dangerous, both to humans and to animals.

All they
knew was
loneliness.

The dogs didn't know their fate. One young dog,
labeled Number 32, waited and waited for someone to
notice him, while another paced nervously at the back of
her cage.

The black puppy now lived in a crowded animal
shelter, with rows of cages stacked on top of one another.
His cage, Number 86, became his name.

No one was supposed to talk to or pet the dogs because they were evidence, but sometimes, late at night, a shelter worker snuck out Number 86 to get a little exercise. Lonely days, then weeks, then months passed.

Luckily for the dogs, some people saw them as victims. They knew that the dogs had been forced to fight. Several animal rights groups—including the ASPCA, Best Friends Animal Society, and the California-based BAD RAP (Bay Area Doglovers Responsible About Pitbulls)—joined together to ask the court to give the dogs a chance at life.

Finally, in early September 2007, the court allowed BAD RAP and the ASPCA to test all forty-nine Vick pit bulls to see if they would be safe to handle.

Nine testers tried to see how the dogs would react to different situations—such as approaching them with a life-size doll to see if children upset them. The testers also needed to see how the Vick dogs would behave around other dogs.

After four long months alone in their cages, many of the dogs—including Number 86—greeted one another with eager play bows and wagging tails. When the testing was done, all but one of the dogs were ruled safe.

The results surprised everyone.

After almost two more months of tests, sixteen Vick dogs were allowed to leave the shelters—including Number 86. On October 21, after a bath and a quick run, he and twelve others traveled across the country in an RV with BAD RAP members Nicole and Steve. At times he would sit in his cage, gazing out the window, the rocking of the van lulling him to sleep. The trip went by quickly.

His new life was about to begin.

Nicole and Steve took Number 86 to their home in San Diego, where he finally got a real name: Dutch. For the first time, he was able to play with toys and romp with Grace, another rescued Vick dog.

Still, Dutch needed a permanent home. After getting to know him better, Nicole and Steve thought he'd be a good fit for their friend Linda. She lived near San Francisco and already had two adopted pit bulls. But she was looking for a new dog to train for agility competition, where dogs run through a series of physical tasks with directions from their handlers. Agility competition requires energy, intelligence, and concentration.

This little guy has as much energy as a whole pack of dogs.

Linda and her husband, Bill, knew Dutch had the energy.
They agreed to take him in for foster care in April 2008, to
see if he had the focus and the smarts.

Another move, another home.

The black puppy needed
to learn how to live in a house
with people and other dogs. He
would jump up onto the dining
table and chew on shoes. Once
he swallowed a sock and needed
emergency surgery, but he
survived. Fortunately, he felt safe
in his denlike crate in the living
room, so Linda could put him
there to keep him out of trouble.

As time passed, Linda noticed Dutch limping after exercise. She took him to the vet, who gave her bad news: Dutch had bad knees and could never be an agility dog unless they were fixed.

Linda felt terribly disappointed. She really wanted to do agility work, but she and Bill had fallen in love with Dutch.

They decided to see if the vet could fix his knees, but whatever happened, Dutch belonged with them.

The little black dog had found his forever home.

Just one thing—Bill an[d]
Linda didn't think the nam[e]
Dutch suited him. Bill sugg[ested]
they name him after the
American war hero Audie
(AW-dee) Murphy, a little [guy]
who had survived a tough
childhood and went on to [win]
more medals during Worl[d]
War II than any other soldi[er]
because of his brains and
bravery. Their new dog wa[s]
like that—small, smart, and
brave.

So Dutch became Aud[ie.]

Even if he couldn't be an agility dog, Audie still
needed to have his knees fixed. Luckily, the court had
ordered Michael Vick to set aside a fund for the dogs.
It paid for Audie's surgery in December 2008.

At first, Audie had to stay in his crate all the
time, except for two short walks a day. Each week,
the walks got longer. Staying in a small space was
frustrating for such an active dog.

Linda put pants on his legs so that he couldn't lick his stitches.

While he recovered, Linda carried him by his harness—
like a big purse—when he had to go down stairs. Little by
little, he got better. Exercises, like balancing on an air-filled
plastic cushion, helped strengthen his healing legs. Bit by bit
he was allowed to go up and down stairs.

Working together on his recovery helped Audie learn to trust and rely on Linda. He was on his way to understanding the life of a beloved pet. But would he ever be strong enough for agility work?

Riding on a skateboard also helped.

Over time, Audie has learned to trust people.

Audie needed training in the company of other dogs. Linda signed up for Canine Good Citizen classes, where dogs learn to obey their people and to behave politely around humans and other dogs.

Training a dog to sit, stay, and greet properly also strengthens the partnership between a dog and its person.

Audie has passed his Canine Good Citizen test!

The good news finally came in April 2009—Audie's knees had healed perfectly, and he would be able to train for agility competition.

Success in agility requires teamwork between a dog and its trainer. The team of dog and person is judged by how well the dog gets through the obstacles and by how much time it takes to finish the course.

Audie is a natural at agility training.

Audie quickly learned to manage the teeter-totter, jump through hoops, and zip through the weave poles. Running through the tunnel is no problem for him either. Once he masters every obstacle, he and Linda will enter fun matches and then real competition.

Every Saturday, Audie joins Linda and other BAD RAP
volunteers to give obedience classes for people with pit bull–type
dogs who want their pets to be good canine companions. The
dogs learn basic commands like sit, stay, and heel, and they learn
how to meet and greet both humans and other dogs politely.

The parking lot is a busy place.

Audie and his friends have come a long way from Bad Newz Kennels. Uba, who was Number 32, lives with his person, Letti, and Daisy, a tan-colored dog rescued from a fighting ring in Oklahoma. He is a happy, beloved pet.

Audie loves to see his Vick dog friends.

Daisy loves
making new friends
with the other Vick
dogs and their people.

Frodo, who had been
shown cowering against a
cinder-block wall during
the testing process, is still
very shy with strangers,
but loves his dog friends
Audie and Uba, who are
nuzzling behind him.

Audie enjoys working with Linda to help other dogs.

People and other dogs helped Audie. Now he helps dogs in Linda's classes learn good behavior when he acts as a "canine coach." He encourages the dogs to feel comfortable around an unfamiliar dog by running around the class with Linda while the others sit quietly.

A neighbor, Kim, asks Linda to help with her shy
German shepherd, Ladybug, who is afraid of other dogs.
Linda and Audie stand still on the sidewalk while Kim
and Ladybug walk by several times. Little by little,
Ladybug's fear will ease if she has good experiences
with other dogs.

Audie enjoys life with his family. BAD RAP has set up a blog for the Vick dogs to tell their stories with the help of their people, and Audie loves to sit with Linda while she writes for it.

Audie's story shows how love and hard work can change a dog's life from one of fear and sadness to one of love and joy.

To read the Vick dogs' blog, go to http://vickdogsblog. blogspot.com.

Pit Bulls

What exactly is a pit bull? This may seem like an easy question, but it isn't. During the nineteenth century, several breeds of dogs were used in dogfights in Great Britain and the United States. They were usually powerful, athletic animals with strong jaws and short coats. They were small enough to be agile and could be picked up easily by humans.

These dogs were also intelligent and very loyal to their people. During the early twentieth century, pit bull–type dogs became a popular family pet in the United States because they were loving, easy to train, and good at guarding against danger. Then, during the 1970s, some people started illegal dogfighting rings, bred the dogs for that purpose, and trained them to fight. As time went by, pit bulls got a bad reputation, and some cities banned them.

While many dogs people call "pit bulls" are not members of any registered breed, there are three official breeds of this type: the American Staffordshire Terrier, which is recognized by the American Kennel Club (AKC); the American Pit Bull Terrier, recognized by the United Kennel Club (UKC) and the American Dog Breeders Association (ADBA); and the Staffordshire Bull Terrier, more popular in the United Kingdom than in America, but still recognized by the AKC and UKC. Audie looks like a typical Staffordshire Bull Terrier, but his background is completely unknown. This breed is especially known for its reliability with children.

BAD RAP

Tim Racer and Donna Reynolds launched BAD RAP on April 1, 1999. They envisioned a local organization of volunteers that would help rescue and foster pit bulls in the San Francisco Bay Area. However, once they launched their website, they received e-mails from across the country asking for information and help related to pit bulls. The website has become a resource for information about pit bulls that's available to everyone, as well as a champion for canine victims of abuse. When the Michael Vick case broke, Donna and Tim recognized the opportunity to change the way dogfighting cases were handled. Because of the publicity surrounding the bust, the public wanted to know what would happen to the dogs that were victims of Bad Newz Kennels. With the help of many dedicated people and organizations, the Michael Vick case has changed the way the legal system deals with dogfighting rings. Dogs that can be rehabilitated now have a chance for a good life.

BAD RAP volunteers help these dogs in many ways—serving as advocates for them in the legal system, providing foster homes for rescued pit bulls, giving information to people about living with pit bulls, teaching classes to Bay Area pit bull owners and their dogs, and more.

The Michael Vick Case Timeline

April 25, 2007—Police and animal control officers raid the Bad Newz Kennels, owned and operated by NFL quarterback Michael Vick. Sixty-six dogs, fifty-one of them pit bulls, are taken as evidence and placed in six animal shelters. Two later die in a shelter.

July 2, 2007—Federal officials rule that a dogfighting operation had been carried out at the site.

July 17, 2007—Michael Vick and three other men are indicted by a grand jury for running the dogfighting ring for six years.

July 26, 2007—Michael Vick pleads not guilty.

July 30, 2007—BAD RAP suggests that the Vick dogs be evaluated for possible adoption.

August 20, 2007—The ASPCA agrees to join BAD RAP in the evaluation process. Only one dog is deemed unsafe and must be put to sleep.

August 24, 2007—The NFL suspends Vick indefinitely.

August 27, 2007—Vick changes his plea to guilty.

October 21, 2007—BAD RAP takes thirteen Vick dogs on a cross-country road trip to begin their journey to a new life.

November 20, 2007—The court orders Vick to pay almost $1 million to cover the expenses for the pit-bull victims.

December 10, 2007—Vick is sentenced to twenty-three months in prison. He ends up serving eighteen months in federal prison in Leavenworth, Kansas, and the remaining months of his sentence under house arrest. Vick has to declare bankruptcy because of lost salary, bonuses, and endorsement deals.

December 17, 2007—BAD RAP is given permanent custody of many of the Vick dogs, and they begin working with the dogs to ultimately allow them to be adopted into their new families.

January 2, 2008—Twenty-two of the Vick dogs, thought to be the hardest to socialize, arrive at the Best Friends Animal Society's sanctuary in Utah.

July 27, 2009—The NFL reinstates Michael Vick, making him eligible to return to the game of professional football.

August 13, 2009—Michael Vick is signed by the Philadelphia Eagles for a one-year, $1.6 million contract—with an option for a second year at $5.2 million.

September 21, 2010—Michael Vick is promoted to starting quarterback for the Philadelphia Eagles.

For Further Reading and Surfing

Animal rescue groups involved with the Vick dog rescue:

BAD RAP (Bay Area Doglovers Responsible About Pitbulls)
http://www.badrap.org
Lots of useful information about pit bulls in general and the Vick dogs in particular, as well as links to resources of many kinds.

ASPCA (American Society for the Prevention of Cruelty to Animals)
http://www.aspca.org
A major organization devoted to animal welfare.

Best Friends Animal Society
http://www.bestfriends.org/vickdogs
A national animal rescue group that was a big part of the Vick dog rescue efforts. Twenty-two of the most abused Vick dogs were brought to Best Friends' sanctuary to live. Visit this site to learn about the efforts to help these dogs overcome their fears and problems—and hopefully find new homes.

Pit bull breeds:

ADBA (American Dog Breeders Association)
http://www.adbadog.com
Focuses mainly on the American Pit Bull

American Staffordshire Terrier
http://www.bulldoginformation.com/american-staffordshire-terrier.html

Staffordshire Bull Terrier
http://www.bulldogbreeds.com/staffordshirebullterrier.html

Puppy-raising advice:

American Kennel Club. *The Complete Dog Book for Kids.* New York: Howell Book House, 1996.

Crisp, Marty. *Everything Dog: What Kids Really Want to Know About Dogs.* Minnetonka, Minnesota: NorthWord Books for Young Readers, 2003.

Whitehead, Sarah. *How to Speak Dog!* New York: Scholastic Reference, 2008.

Whitehead, Sarah. *Puppy Training for Kids.* New York: Barron's Educational Series, 2001.

Canine Good Citizens Program
http://www.akc.org/events/cgc/program.cfm

Can We Help You Keep Your Pet?
http://www.wonderpuppy.net/canwehelp

Agility dog information:

Bonham, Margaret H. *Introduction to Dog Agility.* New York: Barron's Educational Series: 2009

For Linda, Bill, Audie, and Aldo —D. H. P. and W. M.

Acknowledgments

We want to thank everyone who has contributed to making this book possible—our editor, Emily Easton, who conceived the project and guided us so well along the way; the crew at BAD RAP—Linda Chwistek, Kim Geddes, Donna Reynolds, Tim Racer, Nicole Rattay, Kim Ramirez, Letti de Little, and the rest of the gang; Audie's friends by the ferry, Horace J. Stewart, Robert W. Belleau Sr., Phoebe Craig, and Stephanie Davis; his agility trainers, Jennie Keifer and Cynthia Roberts; and Bill Cook and Steve Smith, for loving and caring for Audie as well. Thanks also to Aldo, Audie, Daisy, Elliot, Frodo, Honky Tonk, Ladybug, Lulu, Sally, Uba, and the other dogs whose enthusiastic embracing of life and love have inspired us.

Photo Credits

Linda Chwistek: pages 14 (top), 18, 22–25, back cover
Library of Congress: page 21 (right)
New York Daily News: page 11
Jay Paul: page 10
Nicole Rattay: pages 12, 13 (top), 14 (bottom), 15–17, 19
Richmond Times-Dispatch: page 8
Shutterstock: page 40 (middle and bottom)
All other photographs by William Muñoz

Text copyright © 2011 by Dorothy Hinshaw Patent
Photographs copyright © 2011 by William Muñoz
All rights reserved. No part of this book may be reproduced or transmitted in any form or by any means, electronic or mechanical, including photocopying, recording, or by any information storage and retrieval system, without permission in writing from the publisher.

First published in the United States of America in May 2011 by Walker Publishing Company, Inc., a division of Bloomsbury Publishing, Inc.
www.bloomsburykids.com

For information about permission to reproduce selections from this book, write to Permissions, Walker BFYR, 175 Fifth Avenue, New York, New York 10010

Library of Congress Cataloging-in-Publication Data
Patent, Dorothy Hinshaw.
Saving Audie : a pit bull puppy gets a second chance /
by Dorothy Hinshaw Patent ; photographs by William Muñoz. — 1st ed.
p.   cm.
ISBN 978-0-8027-2272-0 (hardcover) • ISBN 978-0-8027-2273-7 (reinforced)
1. Dog rescue—Anecdotes—Juvenile literature. 2. Animal welfare—Anecdotes—Juvenile literature. 3. Pit bull terriers—Infancy—Anecdotes—Juvenile literature. 4. Vick, Michael, 1980– —Juvenile literature.
I. Muñoz, William, ill. II. Title.
HV4746.P38 2011   636.755'90832—dc22   2010036547

Typeset in Rockwell
Book design by Nicole Gastonguay

Printed in China by Toppan Leefung Printing, Ltd., Dongguan, Guangdong
(hardcover) 10 9 8 7 6 5 4 3 2 1
(reinforced) 10 9 8 7 6 5 4 3 2 1

All papers used by Bloomsbury Publishing, Inc., are natural, recyclable products made from wood grown in well-managed forests. The manufacturing processes conform to the environmental regulations of the country of origin.

LYNNFIELD PUBLIC LIBRARY
LYNNFIELD, MA 01940